Let's Learn About Pockets and Pouches

Using literature books
Go to your library and find simply-written books with large, clear pictures to read aloud to your class. Share as much factual information from these books and other sources as is appropriate for the age, ability, and maturity of your students.

Bibliography

Kangaroos by Beth Wagner; Creative Education, 1991
Kangaroo by Caroline Arnold; Mulberry Books, 1987
Koala by Vincent Serventy; Raintree Childrens Books, 1987
Koala by Caroline Arnold; William Morrow, 1987
Koalas (A Zoobook) by John Bonnett Wexo; Wildlife Education, Ltd., 1988
Koala Lou by Mem Fox; Harcourt Brace Jovanovich, 1988
Meet the Opossum by Leonard Lee Rue; Dodd, Mead, 1983
Peter's Pockets by Judi Barrett; Atheneum, 1974
A Pocket for Corduroy by Don Freeman; Viking Press, 1978
Possum Baby by Bernice Freschet; Putnam, 1978
Possum Magic by Mem Fox; Harcourt Brace Jovanovich, 1983
The Smallest Koala by Errol Broome; Nova, 1988

How to Use
a. Read a page or two aloud to your students.
b. Show any pictures.
c. Discuss what they have heard and seen on those pages.
d. When you have completed a book (or section of a book), check recall of information by asking questions such as:

"What does a _____ like to eat?"
"Where does a _____ live?"
"What does a _____ look like?"
"How is a _____ like you?"

Pockets

It seems that as time passes we have more and more things to carry. In this unit your children will learn about pockets and other types of "carrying" devices we use to solve the problem of getting our personal things from place to place.

Introduction
Guide children in a discussion of pockets and what they are used for. Use questions to lead children to discuss other types of "pockets and pouches" we use to carry our things from one place to another.

Point to a pocket and ask,

"What is that called?"
"What are pockets used for?"
"What kinds of clothes have pockets?"
"Can we carry this in a pocket? Why or why not?"

milk money	ice-cream cone
marbles	house key
cookie	frog

"What else do you have that you can carry your things in?"
(book bag, lunch pail or bag, backpack, etc.)

Explain that some things are too large for a pocket, but still need to be carried safely from place to place. Bring in the actual items whenever possible. Or use the cards on page 3.

baby carrier	briefcase
carpenter's apron	backpack
paper shopping bag	purse

Note: Children match the "pocket or pouch" with what is carried in it.

What Can I Carry?

Note: Children love to hear a favorite story again and again. Read the story below several times practicing a different skill each time you read it.

Peter's Pockets
by Judi Barrett
Atheneum, 1974

Day 1: Read *Peter's Pockets*.

Check children's recall of the story by asking questions such as...
   What are some of the things Peter liked to put in his pockets?
   What did Peter wear that didn't have any pockets?
   How did Peter's mother help Peter have more pockets?
   What did Mother do when his pockets got dirty? wore out?

Day 2: Read *Peter's Pockets*.

Peter could tell what was in his pockets by feeling the outside. Make a set of pockets similar to Peter's (see the last page of the story for a pattern).

a. Put a small object into each pocket. Pin the tops shut so children can't peek inside. Select a child to feel one of the pockets to see what is inside. After the child guesses, open the pocket to verify his/her answer. Continue passing out pockets until everyone has a turn.

b. Send one of the pockets home with each child. Have them return the pocket the next day with a small object in it. Have the children feel each other's pockets and try to guess what is inside.

Day 3: Read *Peter's Pockets*.

a. Review what clothing Peter had that contained no pockets, two pockets, etc.

b. Do the activity "How many pockets do you have?" on page 6.

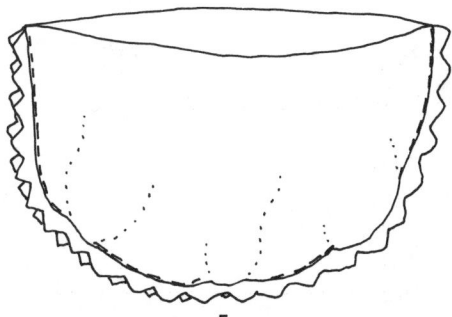

©1995 by Evan Moor Corp.   Pockets and Pouches

People Pockets

How many pockets do you have?

Have your students identify everything they are wearing that has pockets. Have children help each other count how many pockets each child has. Make a simple picture graph to record this information.

1. Reproduce the small pockets on page 8. Give each child one strip of the pockets.

2. Make a chart out of butcher paper containing each child's name.

3. After children figure out how many pockets they have, have them color that amount on their strip of pockets.

4. Each child then cuts out the pockets he/she has colored and brings them up to the recordkeeping chart. The teacher or an aide glues the pockets after the child's name. This creates a simple bar graph.

5. Ask children questions about what the chart shows. Key the questions to the needs of your students.

    "Who has the most pockets?"
    "How many pockets does Amy have?"
    "Does anyone have the same amount of pockets you have?"

If your students are ready to count to large amounts, point to each pocket and have the class count to see how many there are.

What is in your pocket?

Empty Your Pockets
Have children empty their pockets onto their desk. They then list what they have (write or draw) on a paper pocket (see page 10). Combine the items into a class list.

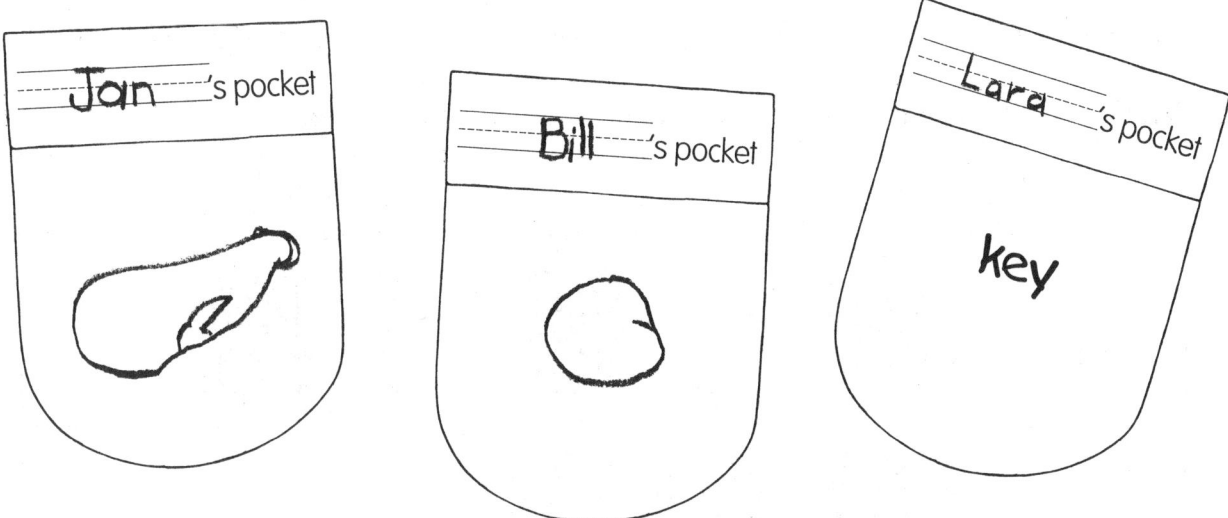

Bonus - sort the items into categories.
        Sort by composition - paper, metal, plastic, etc.
        Sort by use - eat it, play with it, write with it, etc.

A Book of Pockets
Give each person doing the activity a copy of the pocket on page 10. Have children think about something funny or exciting that could be in a pocket. They draw the object, then write a word or sentence about it. Clip the pockets together in a construction paper cover to create a class book for everyone to enjoy.

©1995 by Evan Moor Corp.   Pockets and Pouches

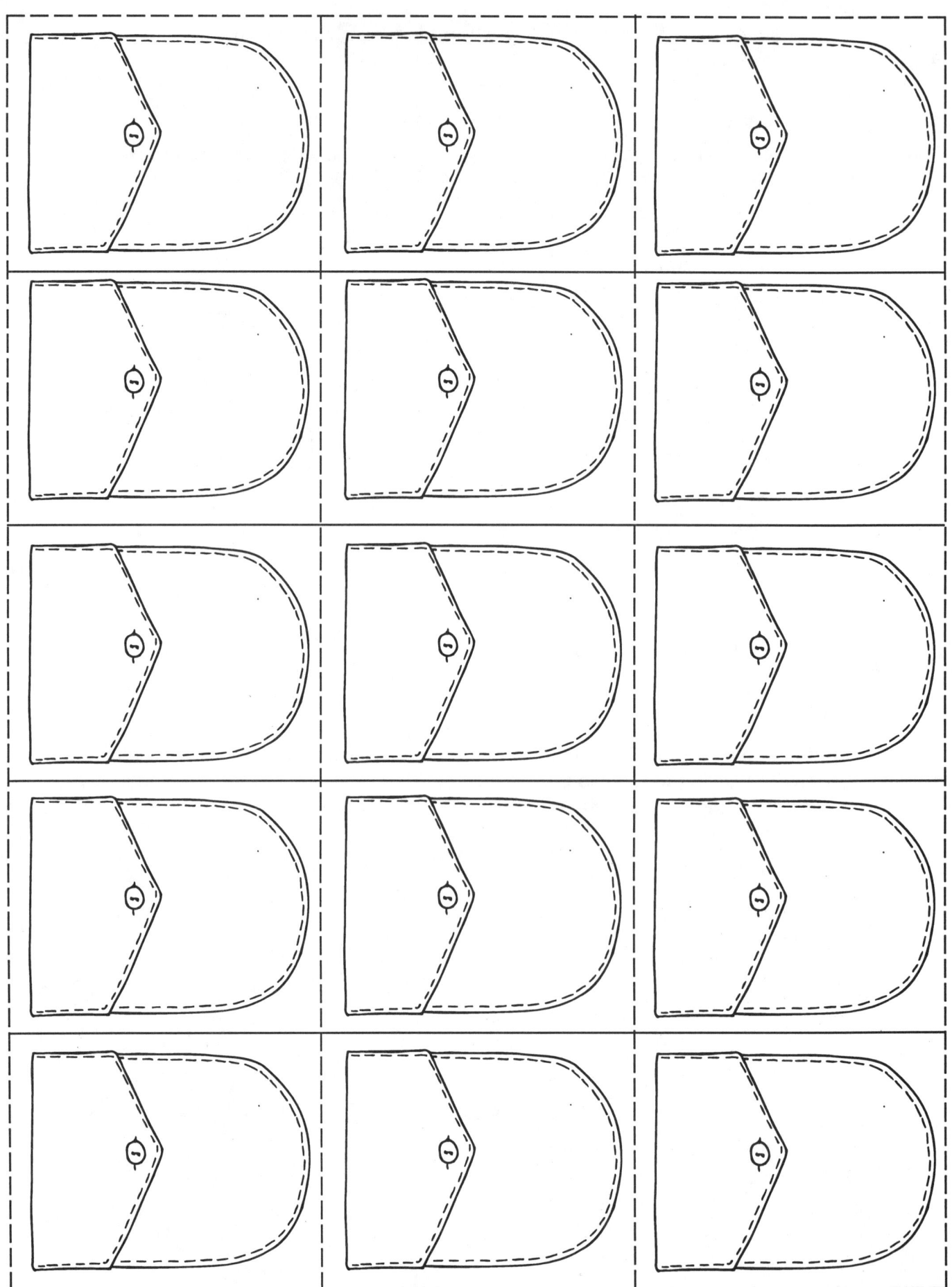

Note: If your students have had a lot of practice with a variety of patterns (abab, abcabc, aabbaa, etc.) you can add additional value to this lesson by requiring their designs to follow a stated pattern.

A Pattern for My Pocket

This activity combines the fun of printing with the excitement of creating an interesting design.

Materials:
- reproduce the pocket pattern (page 10)
- aluminum pie tins
- tempera paint in several colors
- objects to use for printing
  for example:
    - thread spools
    - eraser end of a pencil
    - shapes cut from sponges
    - cookie cutters
- newspaper
- paper towels (for cleaning up spills)

Directions:
1. Cover the work area with newspaper.

2. Place a small amount of paint in each pie tin.

3. Put out the pie tins of paint, the printing objects, and the white paper. (Put the paper supply safely away from the paint containers and printing devices.)

4. Have children work in pairs or small groups. Provide extra newspapers for children to experiment on before they make their final pocket. Children write their names at the top of the page, then print a design on the rest of the pocket. As each pocket is completed, place it aside to dry.

5. Display the completed pockets on a bulletin board for everyone to enjoy. Let each child select something to put in their pockets. This can be a piece of work they have done, a picture from a magazine, their favorite crayon, something from home, etc. Change these frequently.

©1995 by Evan Moor Corp.

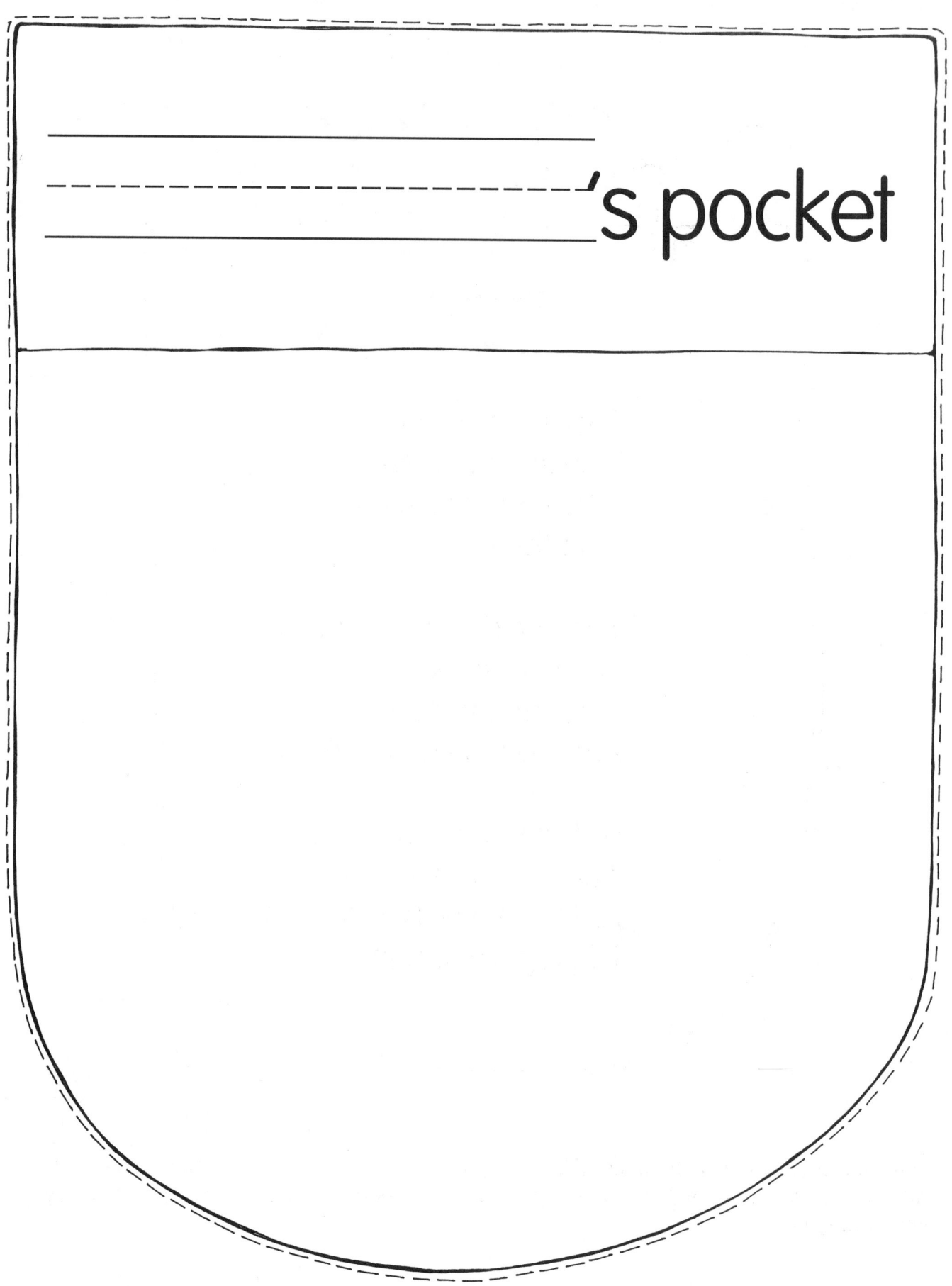

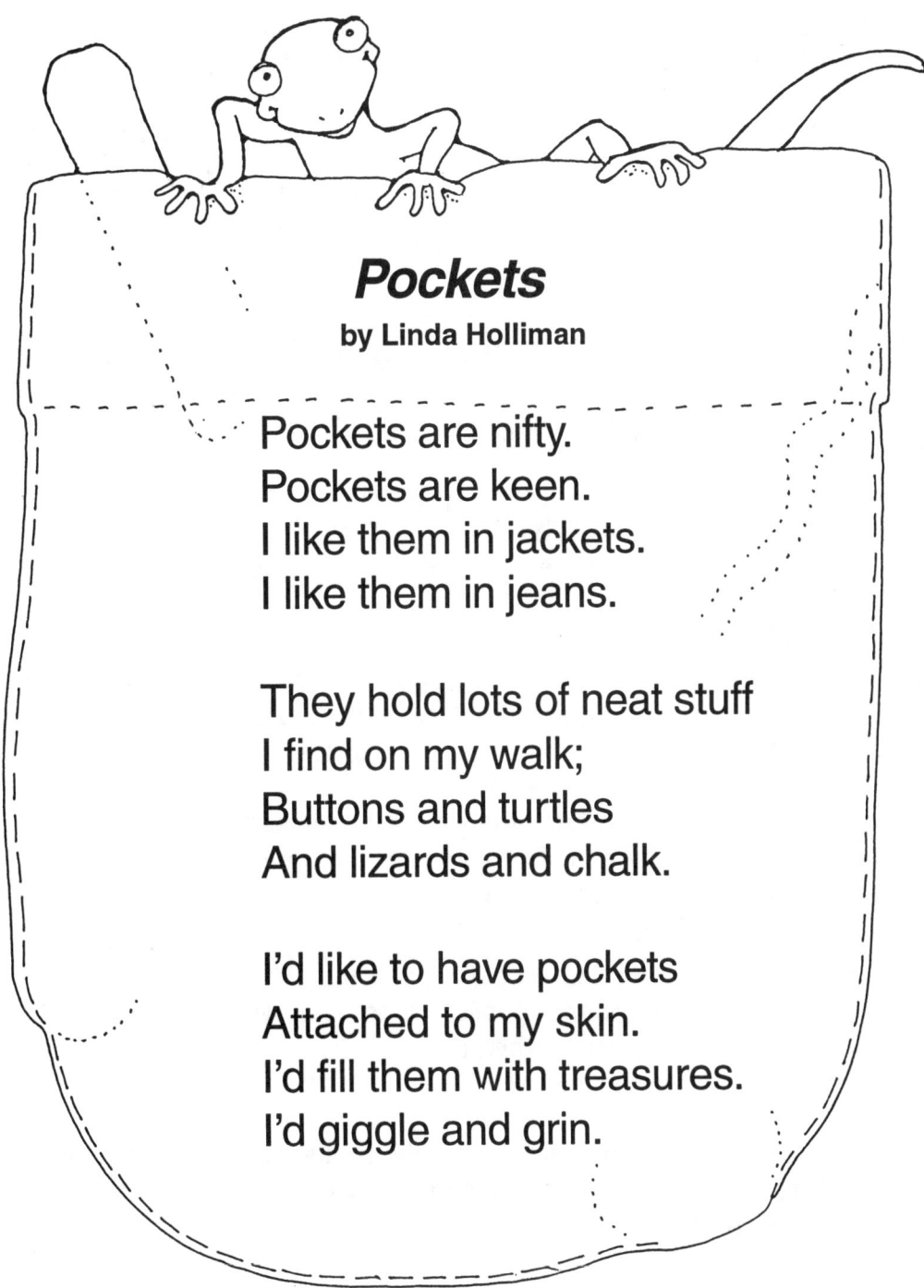

Pockets
by Linda Holliman

Pockets are nifty.
Pockets are keen.
I like them in jackets.
I like them in jeans.

They hold lots of neat stuff
I find on my walk;
Buttons and turtles
And lizards and chalk.

I'd like to have pockets
Attached to my skin.
I'd fill them with treasures.
I'd giggle and grin.

Read this rhyme to your students. Discuss what it would be like to have a permanent pocket attached to your body. Ask children where they would want their skin pocket and what they would carry in it.

Animals with Pouches

Explain that there are special animals that do have pockets. They are called marsupials. Marsupial pockets are called pouches. Explain that these animals have pouches to carry their tiny babies in as they grow. Share the following information with your students. You can best determine how much is appropriate for your specific students.

Reproduce pages 13 - 16 for your students. Staple the pages together in a construction paper cover to create books for children to take home and share with their parents.

Kangaroos
Kangaroos live in Australia. The red kangaroo is the biggest kind of kangaroo. They have big, strong back legs and feet and small front legs and feet. Kangaroos use their big tail for balance as they leap from place to place. Kangaroos eat plants.

Mother kangaroos have pouches. A newborn baby is the size of a lima bean. It crawls into the pouch where it eats, sleeps, and grows. The baby joey lives in the pouch for many months. When it is big enough to come out of the pouch, it still goes back in if there is any danger.

Koalas
Koalas live in Australia in eucalyptus trees. They eat its leaves and sleep in its branches. Koalas only go on the ground to get from one tree to another. Koalas are awake at night and sleep during the day. They wrap themselves around a branch and go to sleep wherever they are.

When koala babies are born, they are about the size of a jellybean. The baby crawls into its mother's pouch where it eats and sleeps. The baby stays in the pouch for many months. When the baby comes out of the pouch it travels around on its mother's back until it is almost grown.

Opossums
Opossums are rat-shaped animals with scaly tails. Opossums live in many countries. They eat leaves, shoots, buds, seeds, and insects. When an opossum is threatened, it "plays possum," pretending to be dead until the danger is over.

Many tiny babies are born at one time. They stay in the mother's pouch eating and sleeping until they grow big enough to come out. Then the mother opossum carries the babies piggy back as she moves from place to place.

Wombats
Wombats live in Australia. They move around on the ground eating grass and the roots of plants. Wombats live in long burrows they dig underground. They have long, bearlike claws that help them dig their burrows and tear up underground roots for food.

Wombats raise their babies in pouches just like kangaroos and koalas. A baby wombat sleeps and drinks milk from its mother in the pouch. It stays in the pouch for about three months.

Kangaroos

Musk Rat-kangaroo

Red Kangaroo

Tree Kangaroo

Here are some kangaroos.
Mother kangaroos have a pouch.

Koalas

Here are some koalas.

Mother koalas have a pouch.

Opossums

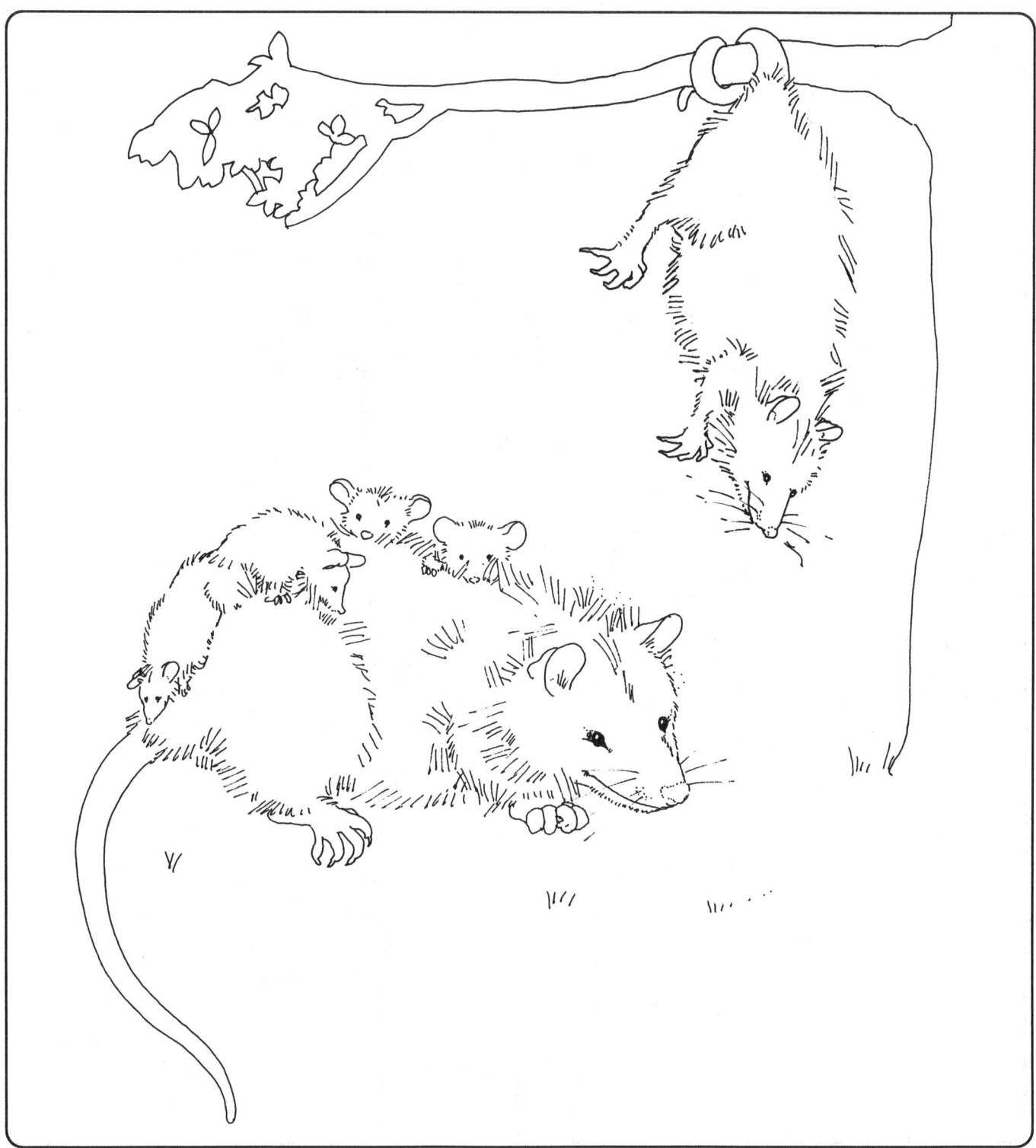

Here are some opossums.

Mother opossums have a pouch.

Wombats

Here are some wombats.

Mother wombats have a pouch.

What do you Remember?

Use the stick puppets on page 18 to check recall of facts about kangaroos, koalas, and opossums. Each child will need one set of puppets. Children answer your questions by showing the correct stick puppet.

1. I hold onto a tree branch when I sleep. Who am I?
   (koala)
2. I have a long, scaly tail like a rat. Who am I?
   (opossum)
3. I use my strong tail to help me balance when I leap. Who am I?
   (kangaroo)
4. I use my sharp claws to dig my burrow. Who am I?
   (wombat)
5. My baby is called a joey. Who am I?
   (kangaroo)
6. I eat grass and the roots of plants. Who am I?
   (wombat)
7. I have big furry ears and a big nose. Who am I?
   (koala)
8. I hop from place to place with my strong legs. Who am I?
   (kangaroo)
9. I play dead if I am scared. Who am I?
   (opossum)
10. I live in a eucalyptus tree. Who am I?
    (koala)
11. I carry all my babies on my back when I go for a walk. Who am I?
    (opossum)
12. I have a pouch where my baby sleeps, drinks milk, and grows. Who am I?
    (all of the marsupials)

Putting Puppets Together
Have children color, cut-out, and paste the puppets on page 18 to ice cream-sticks.

©1995 by Evan Moor Corp.

Note: Share this poem with your students, then guide them through the sequencing activity on page 20.

Mrs. Kangaroo
Has a small surprise
Hiding in her pouch
Away from watching eyes.

A teeny, tiny joey
Growing day by day,
Sleeping and eating
'Til it's big enough to play.

Jo Ellen Moore

Note: Children will need a strip of construction paper 6" x 18" (15.2 x 45.7 cm). They cut the pictures apart and glue them in order along the paper strip.

A Kangaroo is Born

©1995 by Evan Moor Corp.

Note: Share this poem with your students, then guide them through the art activity on pages 22 and 23.

1 koala taking a ride.

2 koalas trying to hide.

3 koalas playing merrily.

4 koalas sleeping in a tree.

5 koalas eating leaves for lunch.

Furry koalas - what a clever bunch.

Jo Ellen Moore

Koalas Live in Trees

Remind children that koalas live in trees, only coming down to run to a new tree. Ask children to name other animals that live in trees (squirrels, birds, etc.).

Koala and Baby in a Tree

Materials for koalas
- copies of the mother and baby on page 23
- glue
- crayons
- scissors

Directions for Koala
Have children make koala bears using the pattern on page 23.
1. Children color the koala parts.
2. Cut out the pieces.
3. Glue the head on the mother koala.
4. Glue the baby on the mother's back.

Older children may be ready to paint their own bears rather than do this cut-and-paste activity.

Materials for the tree
- blue butcher paper
- brown construction paper or brown paper shopping bags
- green construction paper

Directions for Bulletin Board
Cover the bulletin board with blue butcher paper. Create a eucalyptus tree from construction paper. Cut long, thin leaves from green paper and make a trunk from brown construction paper or brown shopping bags. Put the tree together following the steps below. If you are fortunate enough to have a real eucalyptus tree nearby, use real branches instead.

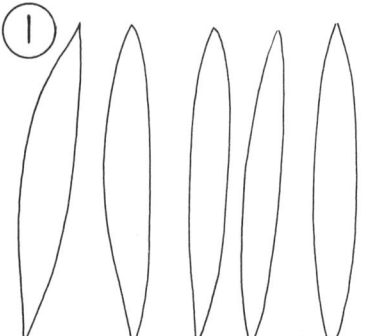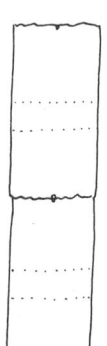

Put the completed koalas on the eucalyptus tree. You can extend this activity by changing the number of koalas in the tree every few days. Ask the children to count as a group as you touch each koala.

©1995 by Evan Moor Corp.   Pockets and Pouches

Koala and Baby

Color. Cut out. Paste.

Note: Children love to hear a favorite story again and again. Read the story below several times practicing a different skill each time you read it.

Possum Magic
by Mem Fox
Harcourt Brace Jovanovich, 1983

Day 1: Read *Possum Magic*.

Ask questions about the story to see how much your students remember. For example...
- Who was Hush?
- Who did she live with?
- What was special about Hush?
- How did Hush become invisible?
- Why did Grandma Poss make Hush invisible?
- Why did Hush want to become visible again?

Day 2: Read *Possum Magic*.

Hush ate many things on her travels around Australia trying to become visible again. Explain to your students what these different foods were (see the last page of the story).

a. Hush ate the same things every year on her birthday to make sure she didn't become invisible again. Ask your students to think about what they would like to eat on their birthday and why they chose those foods. Have them draw pictures of the foods, then provide time for them to share their drawing and reasons for wanting that food with their classmates.

b. If you have helpful parents, ask a few to make "Pavlova" or "Lamington" for your children to sample.

Day 3: Read *Possum Magic*.

One of Grandma Poss' magic spells was to make wombats blue and kookaburras pink. Give your students copies of page 25. Have them find the hidden wombats and color them blue and the hidden kookaburras and color them pink.

wombat

kookaburra

Mrs. Wombat, Mrs. Opossum,
And Mrs. Kangaroo
All of you have nice soft pouches –
And Mrs. Koala too.

Please tell me what it's like to have
A pocket without a shirt
A nice safe place to keep your young
So they will not get hurt.

Do you like to hide things?
Or use it as a vase?
I'll bet that all your children say
That it's their favorite place.

I'd like to have a pocket
Very similar to yours
A place to keep my treasures
When I play outdoors.

What I'd keep inside my pouch
Would be something new to you
I'd probably keep rocks and gum,
A nickel and some glue.

I never know what I might need
When I go out to play,
Maybe just some juice and snacks
Then I'd be fine all day.

Cheryl Kashata

Find the wombats and kookaburras hiding here.

Note: Teach your students this action rhyme about a wombat, then have them put together the puzzle on page 27.

Wombat, wombat turn around.
Wombat, wombat touch the ground.

Wombat, wombat show your toes.
Wombat, wombat rub your nose.

Wombat, wombat dig, dig, dig.
Wombat, wombat dance a jig!

Wombat Puzzle

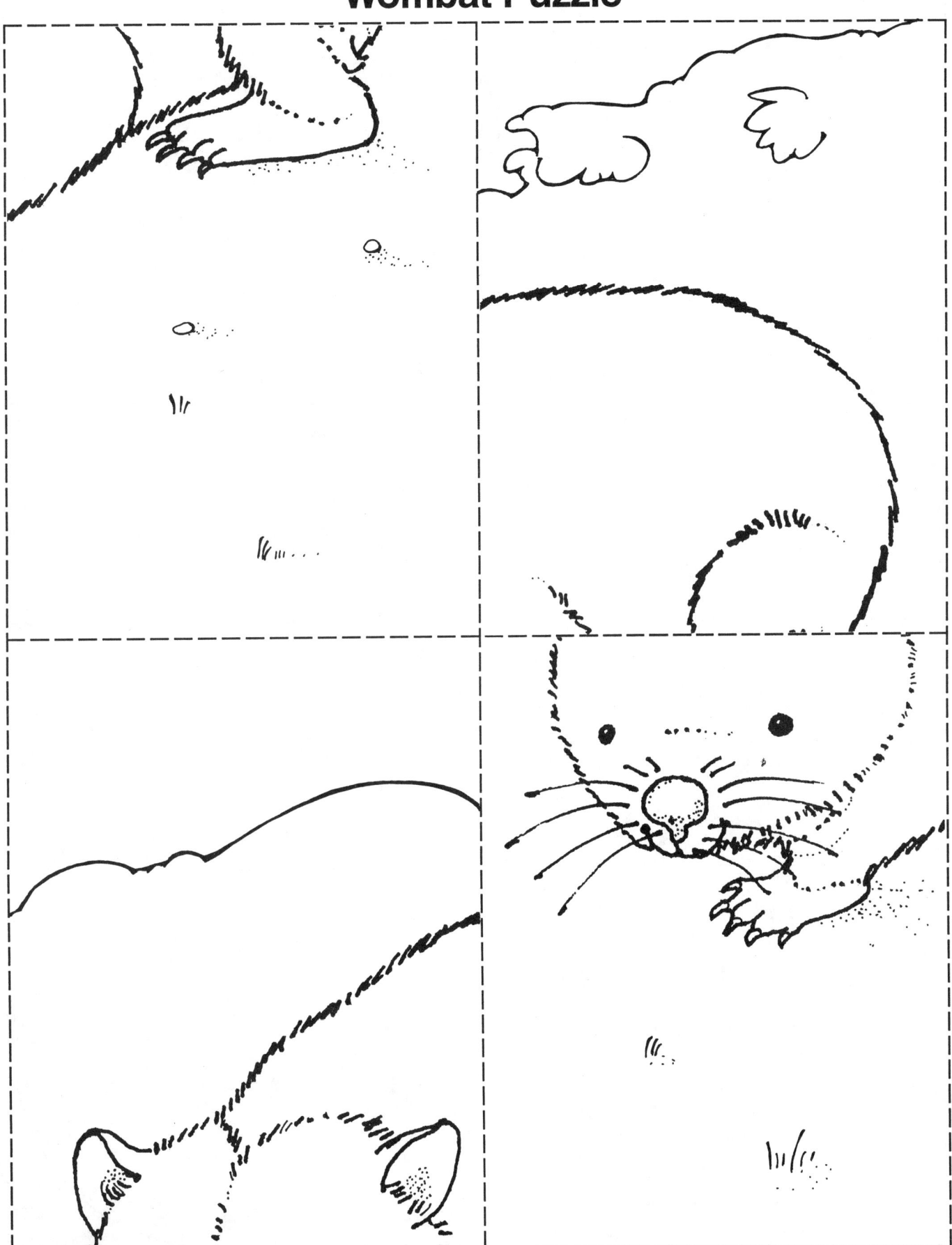

Marsupial Book

- Reproduce pages 28 – 30 for each child making the marsupial book.
- Children color the pictures and complete the sentence at the bottom of the page.
- Arrange the pages in order and staple them together on the left-hand side to complete the book.

Animals with Pouches
by

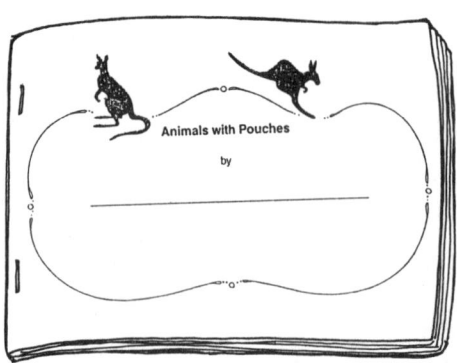

Animals with Pouches
by

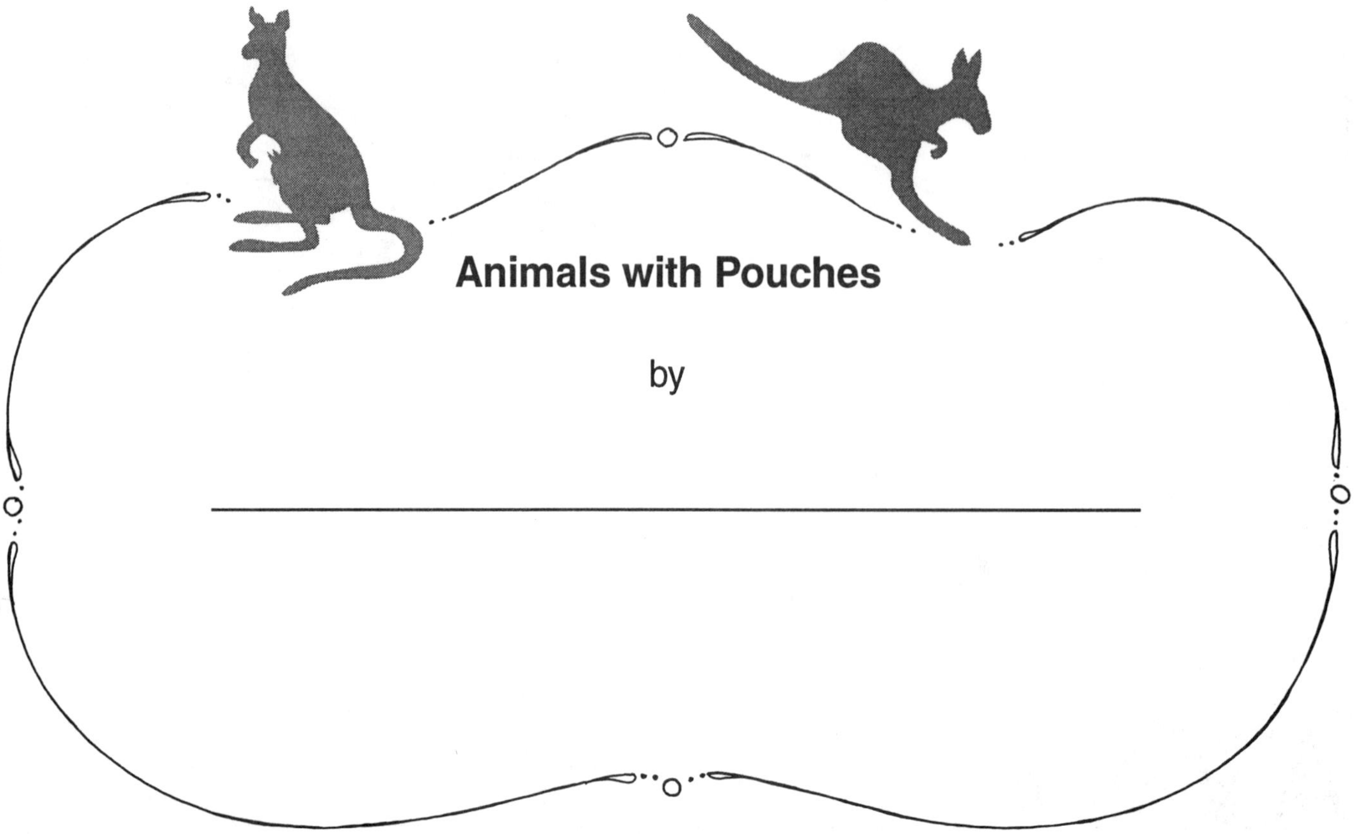

A kangaroo _____

A koala _____

An opossum _____

A wombat _____

What is in this Pocket?

Language Activities

The Sounds Letters Make

1. Listen for initial and final sounds.

    k is for ....

kangaroo	sack
koala	tick
kite	rock
kitten	talk
kettle	skunk

    p is for ....

pocket	cup
pickle	rip
popcorn	top
puppy	stop
pink	map

2. What sound is in my pocket?
   Make a book of the sounds you study. Reproduce the pocket form on page 10. Give each child a copy. Have the child write the letter that makes the sound, then find a picture in a magazine or draw a picture of an item that starts with the sound being studied. Collect the pages and staple them in a cover cut from construction paper. Put the book in your class library for everyone to enjoy.

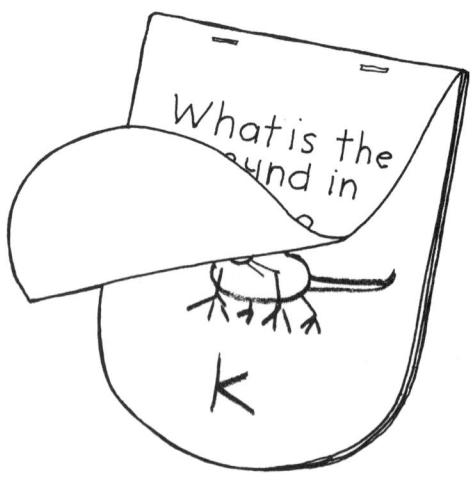

Echo
Use the "Echo" game to practice listening and speaking skills. Children listen carefully to what is being said, then try to repeat it correctly. Begin with single words and work up to sentences containing several words.

words	phrases	sentences
pocket	baby opossum	Ten baby opossums take a ride.
kangaroo	pennies in my pocket	A mob of kangaroos ate the grass.
koala	catch the cute koala	
opossum	a mob of leaping kangaroos	

Using Picture Cards

Vocabulary

1. What is my name?
   Reproduce the picture cards on page 34. Show each picture and teach the name of the animal illustrated.

   Follow these steps to check recall. Show one card. Call on a child to name the animal. Display three cards. Name one of the animals. Select a child to find the animal you named.

2. What do I look like?
   a. Marsupials - Use the same picture cards you reproduced for the preceding activity. Teach words that describe the marsupials by color, body covering, size, etc. Show one card at a time. Have your students describe the marsupial. You may need to model the activity. For example, "This is a koala. It has gray hair. It has a big nose. You can see its sharp claws."

   b. Pockets - Use the pocket pattern cards on page 35. Discuss the colors, patterns, and sizes of the pockets. Display three (or more) cards. Describe one of the pockets shown. Children must decide which card shows that pocket. Vary the activity by having a child do the describing. Model the activity for your students. "I see a big pocket with polka dots."

Alike and Different

Show two of the marsupial cards and ask your students to tell how the animals are alike. Vary the activity by asking children to tell you the differences.

Visual Memory

These activities can be done using the marsupial cards or the pocket pattern cards.

1. Find the Missing Picture
   Display several cards. Discuss what each card shows. Have your students shut their eyes as you remove one card. They open their eyes and try to decide which card has been removed. The more cards you use, the more challenging the activity becomes.

2. All in a Row
   Display several cards. Discuss what each card shows and the order it comes in. Have your students close their eyes as you rearrange the order. Students open their eyes and try to put the cards back in the original order.

Reproduce the picture cards. Color, laminate, and cut them apart. Use the cards with the activities on page 33.

©1995 by Evan Moor Corp. Pockets and Pouches

Reproduce the picture cards. Color, laminate, and cut them apart.
Use the cards with the activities on page 33.

©1995 by Evan Moor Corp. 35 Pockets and Pouches

Movement Activities

How Do I Move?
Pantomime the movements of various marsupials.

- Hop like a kangaroo.
- Climb like a koala or tree kangaroo.
- Dig like a wombat.
- "Play possum" like an opossum.

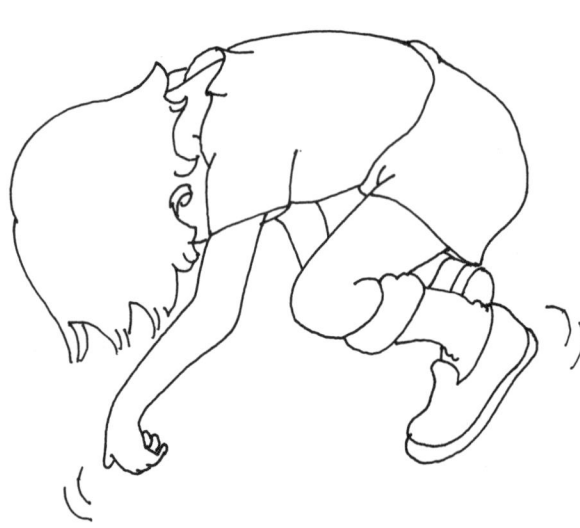

Kangaroo Hop
This is best done outside where you have plenty of room to move about. Explain and demonstrate how a kangaroo hops (two feet together as it takes off and lands). Have children practice hopping around in the correct manner, then do one or more of the following activities.

1. Have children hop from one place to another. "Hop from the sandbox to the grass." Adjust the distance to the ability of your students.

2. Make a pathway with masking tape. Have children hop like a kangaroo along this path.

3. Kangaroos are great jumpers. Have children hop over simple obstacles. This can be two pieces of masking tape placed a short distance apart or a low obstacle such as a wooden building block. (If you use an obstacle, have children do the activity in a sandbox or on the grass in case someone falls.)

©1995 by Evan Moor Corp.   Pockets and Pouches

Catch the Opossum

Play this game on the lawn since children may lay down to "play possum" at some point. It is a variation of "tag."

Limit the space in which children can run in some way (long jump ropes used to outline a large circle for example). Choose one person to be "It." This person is going to try to catch one of the opossums. Emphasize that the "opossum" is to be touched gently, not grabbed. As long as a child is moving, he/she can be tagged. If the child "plays possum" by freezing in place or laying down playing dead, he/she is safe. If an "opossum" is tagged, he/she becomes "It."

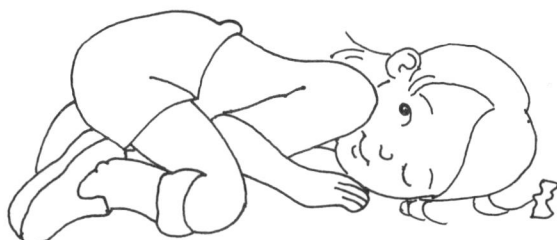

Put it in the Pouch

Make several kangaroo beanbags by writing the word "joey" on them with permanent marking pen. Enlarge the kangaroo on page 19 on butcher paper using an opaque projector. Tape the kangaroo to a wall and set a waste basket in front of it to serve as a "pouch."

Place a piece of masking tape on the floor a short distance from the basket pouch. (This distance can be increased as children become more proficient.) Children take turns trying to get the joey into the pouch. Watching children at this task will give you information about motor control.

Math

How Many Opossum Babies?

Make the pattern pieces on pages 39 and 40 from felt or Pellon to use on your flannel board. Make one baby opossum for each number you are practicing. Glue the two parts of the mother opossum together.

1. **Counting Sets**
   Place a set of babies on the mother's back (as though they were riding "piggyback"). Ask "How many babies are going for a ride?" Continue practicing by changing the number of babies and asking the same question.

2. **Reading Numerals**
   Write the numerals on the baby opossums. Place the babies in order one at a time on the mother's back. Ask children to read the number for you. When your students are comfortable doing this, mix the numbered babies up on the side of the board. Select a child to find the number which should come first and place it on the mother's back near the head. Keep selecting children to locate the next number until all of the babies are riding on mother's back.

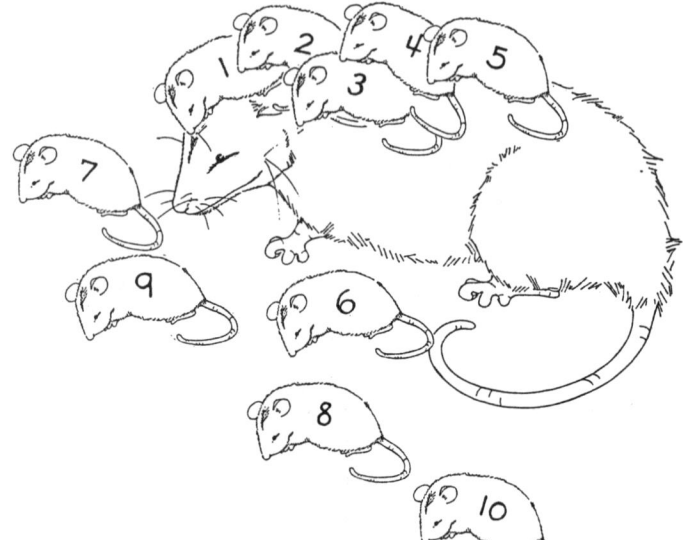

End the lesson by having children sing this rhyme as you point to each baby.

    1 little, 2 little, 3 little opossums,
    4 little, 5 little, 6 little opossums,
    7 little, 8 little, 9 little opossums,
    10 opossums in a row.

Remove the babies one at a time as you sing the song in reverse.

    10 little, 9 little, 8 little opossums,
    7 little, 6 little, 5 little opossums,
    4 little, 3 little, 2 little opossums,
    1 opossum left to go.

Opossum Patterns

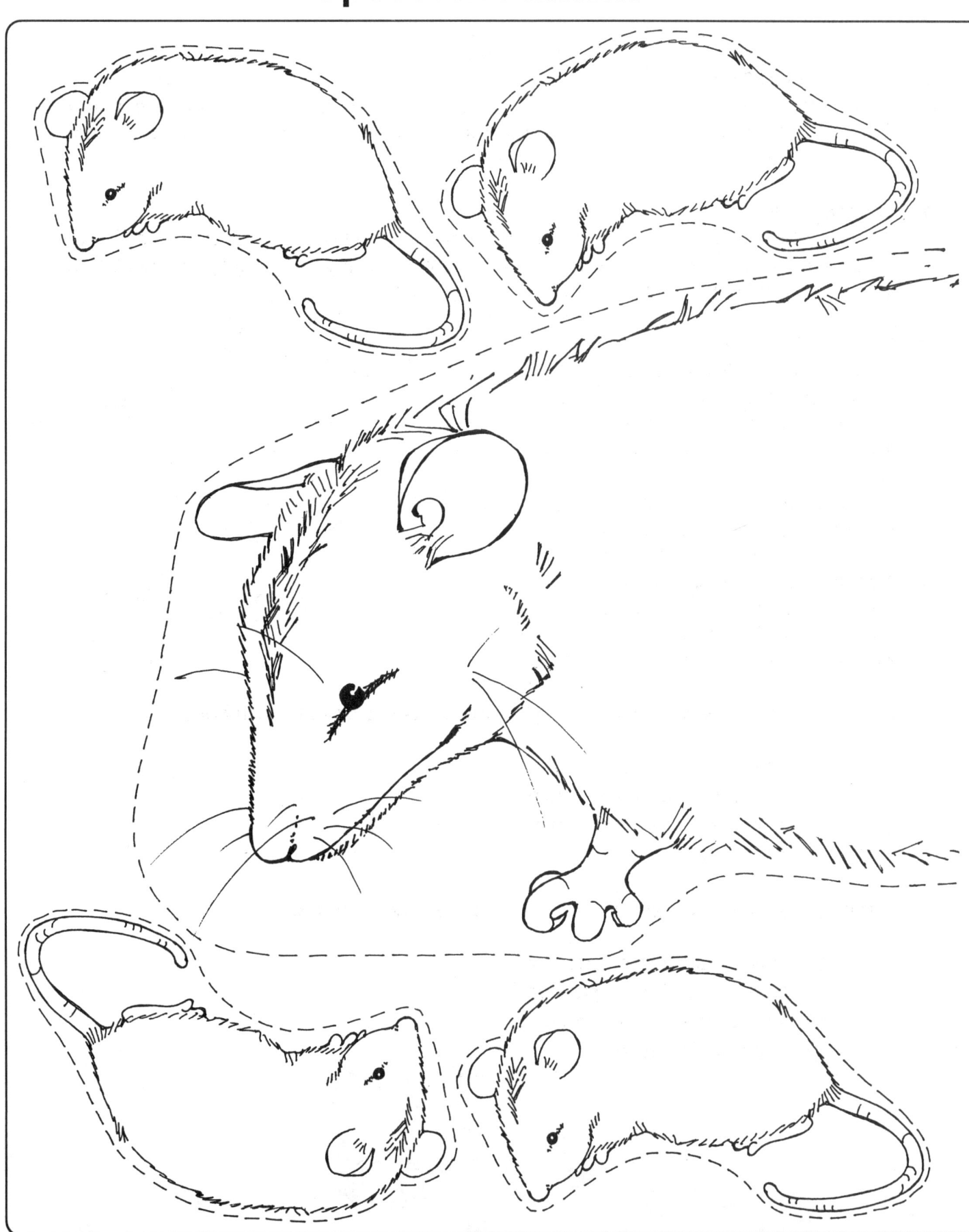

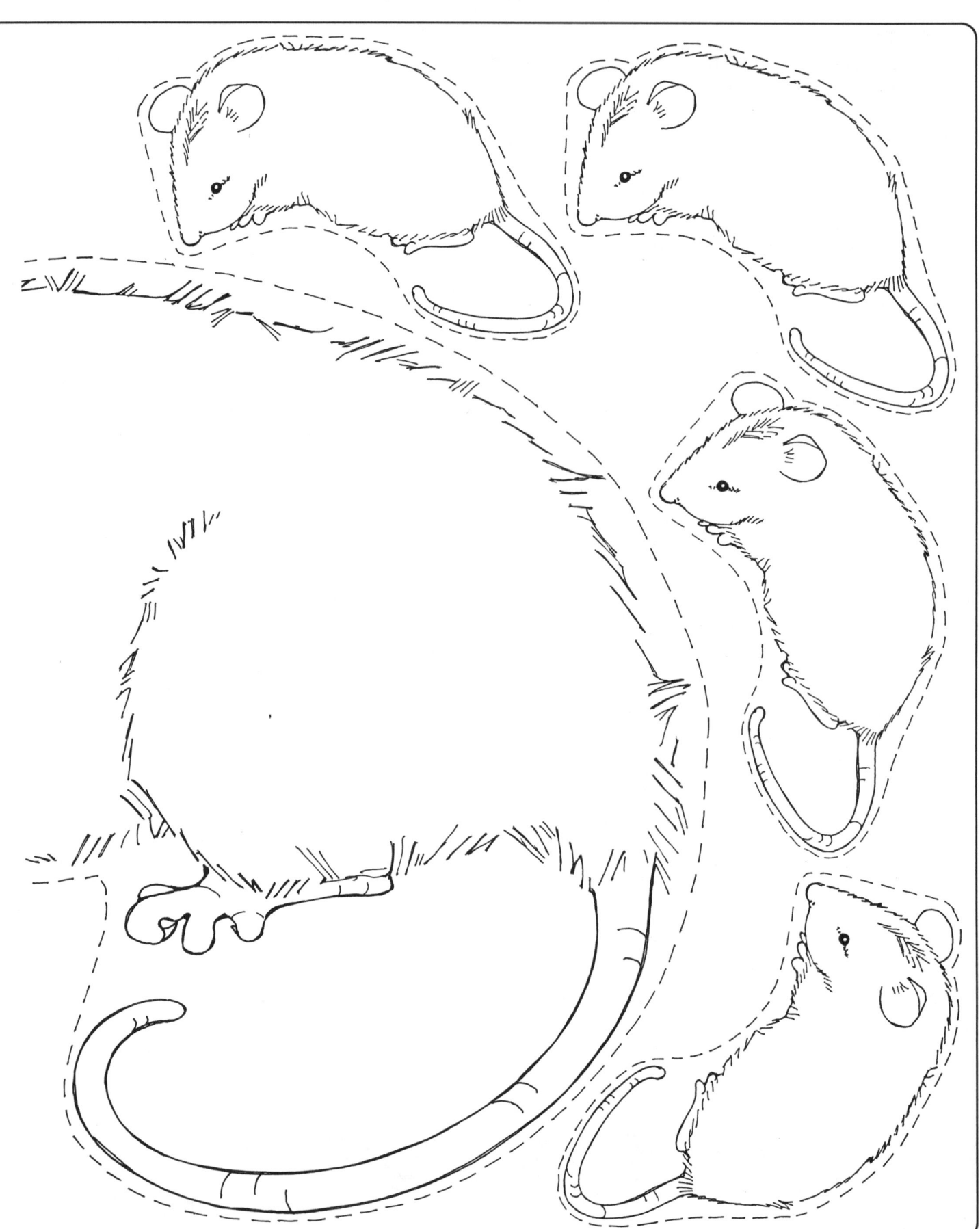

Patterning

Reproduce the patterns of koalas, kangaroos, opossums, and wombats on page 43 to use for patterning practice.

Use one marsupial in several colors or use all of the marsupials in the same color to create your patterns.

1. Lay out a pattern. Have children copy the pattern exactly. Begin with simple patterns. Create more complicated ones as they are able to succeed with the simple ones.

2. Lay out a pattern. Have children continue the pattern.

3. Have children create a pattern for their classmates to copy.

Feed the Hungry Koala

Make several koalas out of felt or Pellon to use with this activity (see page 43). Make several long, thin leaves from green felt or Pellon colored green with a permanent marking pen.

1. Place one koala on the flannel board. Put __(two)__ leaves by the koala. Ask "How many leaves did the hungry koala eat?" Repeat with other quantities of leaves.

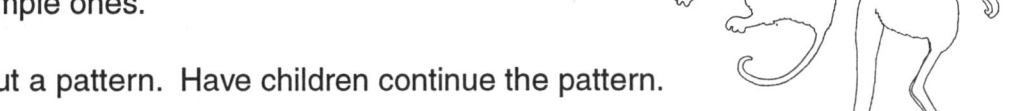

2. Place several koalas on the board. Ask "How many leaves will you need to give each hungry koala one leaf?" Select a student to come up and place one leaf by each koala. Have the group count each leaf as it is placed by the koala. If your students are ready to practice counting by twos, ask "How many leaves will we need to give each hungry koala two leaves?"

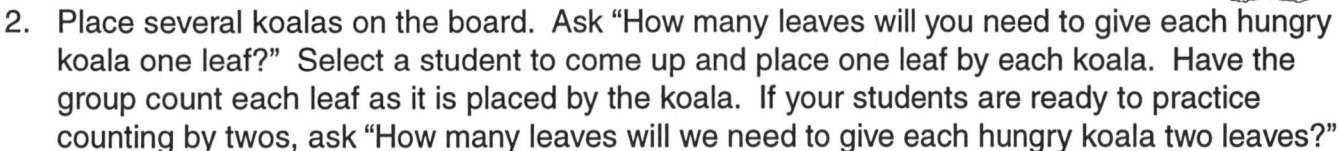

3. Place a koala on the board. Ask a child to come up and "feed" the koala a stated number of leaves. Repeat to practice the numbers one to ten.

How Many Kangaroos in a Mob?

Reproduce several kangaroos (see page 43) from brown felt or Pellon colored with permanent marking pen.

1. Put several kangaroos close together on the flannel board. Have your students count the kangaroos and tell you how many are in the "mob." Repeat with other amounts of kangaroos.

2. Say a number. Select a child to put that many kangaroos on the board. (Repeat several times.)

3. Put __(two)__ kangaroos on the flannel board. Ask, "How many kangaroos will be in the mob if one more hops in?" "How many kangaroos will be in the mob if one hops away?" After each question, select a child to add or take away kangaroos to verify your students' answers. If your children are ready to read and write equations, write each problem on the chalkboard as you state it. Write the answer once it has been given and verified.

How far can you hop?

Have each child pretend to be a kangaroo and see how far they can jump. Do this on the lawn or in the sandbox in case someone falls. If children are ready for standard measurement, use a yardstick or measuring tape to measure the distance. If they are still using non-standard measurement, cut out a paper "kangaroo foot" and use this to see how many kangaroo feet they can jump. Remind them that a kangaroo jumps with both feet together.

Patterns for Patterning

Put it in a Pocket

Make a "pocket shirt" or "pocket apron" to use with the following activities. Take a large apron or shirt. Sew on many pockets of different sizes, colors, designs, and textures from old clothing. If you put a Velcro dot on each one, you can add letters or numbers to extend the use of your pockets.

1. Pick a Poem:
   Put a poem or rhyme in each pocket. Children can pick a pocket to choose a poem for you to read to them.

2. What's in My Pocket?

   a. Place small objects beginning with sounds or letters you are studying in each pocket. Point to a pocket and ask a riddle.

      "It starts with p. It is an animal that lives on a farm. It says oink. What is in my pocket?" (a pig)

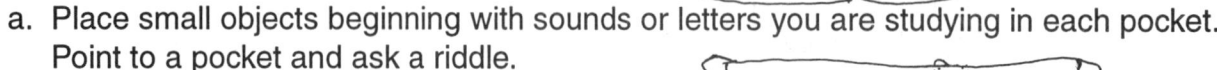

   b. Put a felt letter on each pocket. Put an object beginning with the sound shown into each pocket. Have children find the correct pocket and give you the object they find inside.

      "Find the pocket with the letter that says k. What is in the pocket?"
      (a kangaroo)

   c. Put a felt letter on each pocket. Pass out small objects beginning with those sounds. Have each child find the pocket in which his/her object should go.

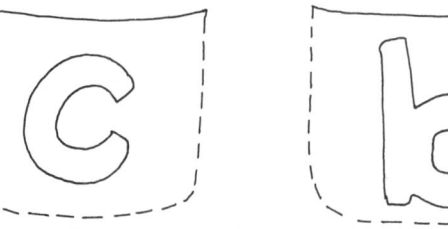 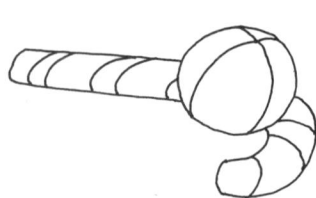

Variation:
Put numerals on the pockets to practice number recognition and counting.

Note: Children love to hear a favorite story again and again. Read the story below several times practicing a different skill each time you read it.

Katy No-Pocket
by Emmy Payne
Houghton Mifflin Company, 1972

Day 1: Read *Katy No-Pocket*.

Help children recall details from the story by asking who, what, when, where, why, and how questions about the story.

Day 2: Read *Katy No-Pocket*.

Say, "The man kept his hammer and nails and tools in the apron full of pockets. If you had his pocket apron, what would you carry in the pockets?"

Reproduce page 46. Have children draw their own faces above the apron, then draw one object they would carry in the pockets. You may need to model the activity by drawing an apron on the board and putting your own pictures in the pockets.

Day 3: Read *Katy No-Pocket*.

Explain that only mother kangaroos have pockets. Make a standing "father" kangaroo following the directions on pages 47 and 48.

Note: Use this form with the activity on page 45.

In Katy's Pockets

Kangaroos

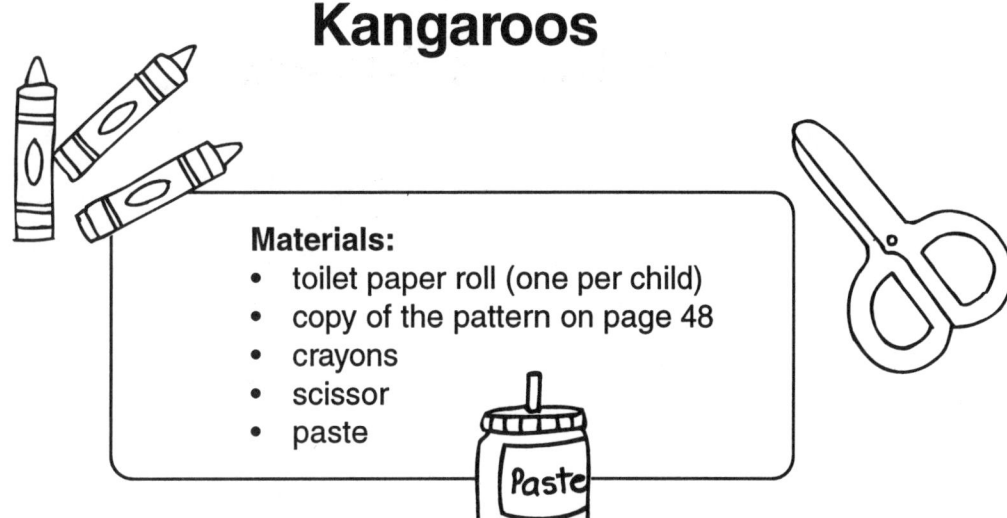

Materials:
- toilet paper roll (one per child)
- copy of the pattern on page 48
- crayons
- scissor
- paste

Directions:
Children color and cut out the pieces, then glue them to the paper tube as shown below.

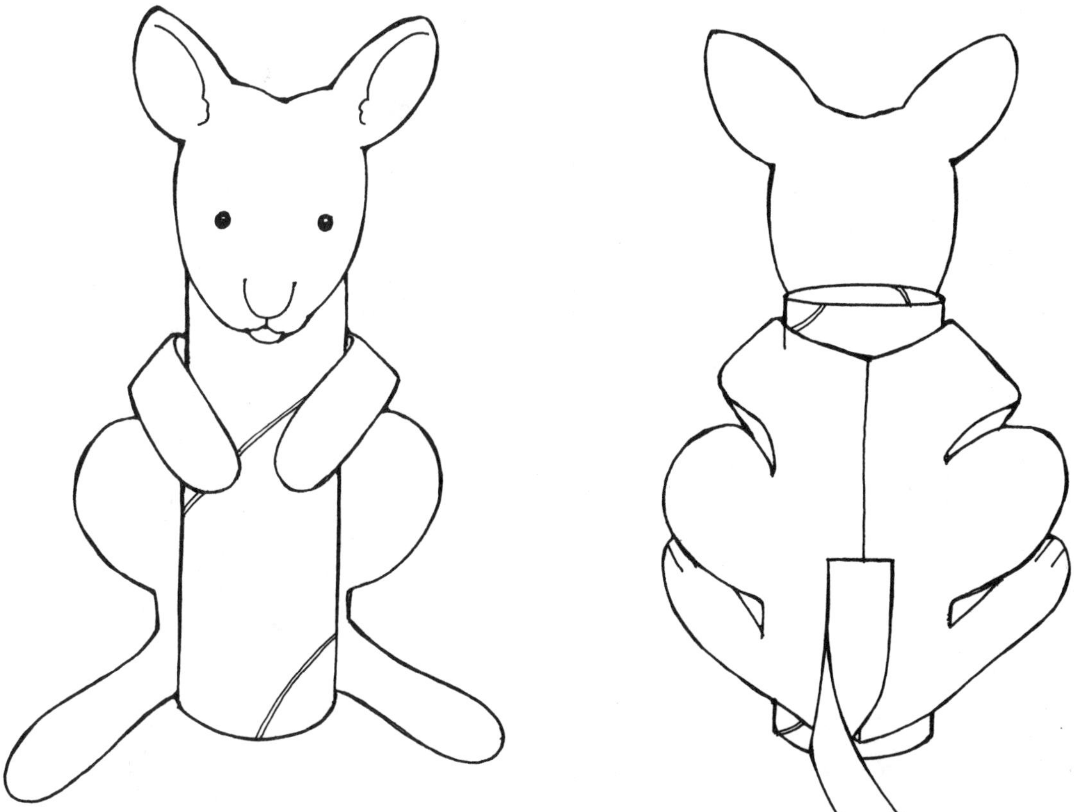

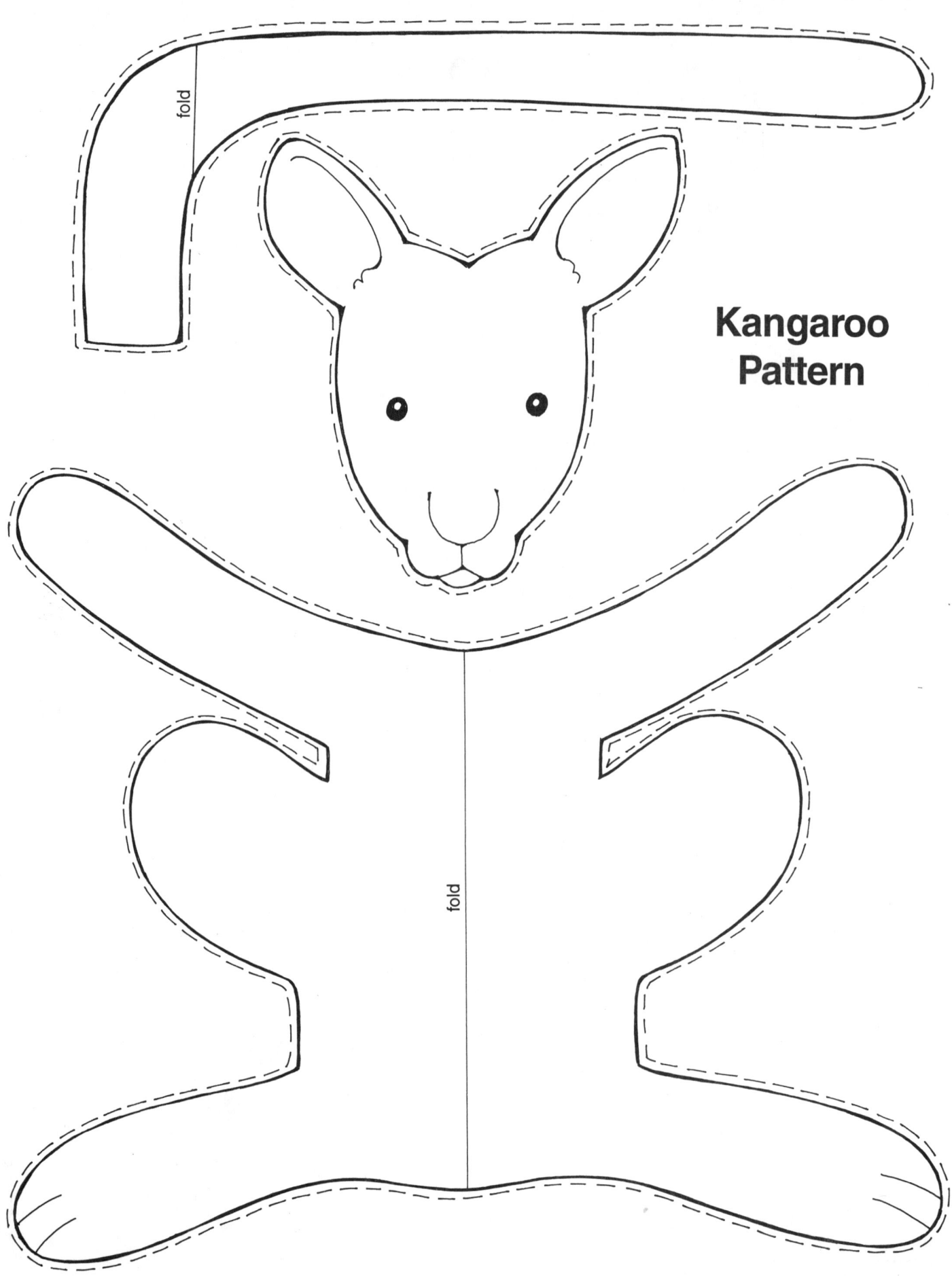